MY
TRUTH

DON BENJAMIN

Don Benjamin
My Truth
Edited by: Jerra Mitchell
Published by: Don B, INC

ISBN: 978-1-7351288-0-1

10 9 8 7 6 5 4 3 2 1

Printed in the United States of America

Note: This book is intended only as a real-life testimony of the life and times of
Don Benjamin. Readers are advised to consult a professional before making any
changes in their life. The reader assumes all responsibility for the consequences of
any actions taken based on the information presented in this book. The information
in this book is based on the author's research and experience. Every attempt has been
made to ensure that the information is accurate; however, the author cannot accept
liability for any errors that may exist. The facts and theories about life are subject to
interpretation, and the conclusions and recommendations presented here may not
agree with other interpretations.

CONTENTS

INTRODUCTION. 1

1   IT'S AT THE ROOT 5

2   YOU'RE THE FRUIT 13

3   HURT PEOPLE HURT PEOPLE 21

4   FORGIVE. 33

5   LETTER TO MY DAD 39

6   MAKE A CHOICE. 43

7   DEAR FUTURE WIFEY 53

8   BE THE MAN YOU WISH RAISED YOU. 57

9   GET HELP 63

10 YOU ARE THE MASTER OF YOUR OWN LIFE. 72

11 THE SPOTLIGHT IS BRIGHT 79

12 YOUR BOYS CAN WAIT 87

13 LETTER TO GOD. 93

INTRODUCTION

It's 1am on March 18, 2020 - the first day of the COVID-19 lockdown in LA. I'm laying down on my mom's couch scrolling thru Instagram, bored out of my mind, and it hit me. *I want to write my first book!* I want to let people in on my life and my journey. Not only that, I want to use my voice to help as many people as I know possible. You're probably wondering, "Help with what?" Well, I want to help the so-called men in the world really become MEN! To help every guy out there really reach MANHOOD. Not just help the men, I also want the women to know it's possible for a guy to pull his own head out of his butt, get it together, and be a man. There is hope ladies. I want to give you a glimpse of my life. The struggle, the glory, the pain I've felt, and the pain I've caused. The wins, and the losses. My interpretation of what it is really like to step up and be a MAN.

Now, I'm pretty sure most people that follow me on social media don't know my story at all, or may not ever care to. Other people may not even have a clue who I am, other than a familiar face in the media. Most people see a fashion model and have no idea the journey it took to get where I am. You're probably thinking, "What kind of journey does it take to become a model? You look good your whole life, then you start modeling. If only it were that easy." You know what is funny? I've literally had people tell me, "Don't say anything. Just sit there and look pretty." That's insensitive as hell, right? All good...but you know what, that's not me, God has put a bigger purpose on my life, and I've known it since as far back as I can remember. Purpose to me isn't just what we choose to do in our career, but instead what we choose to do with our lives that will impact the world with who we become in our career. As a kid, I knew for a fact I would become a professional basketball player. Quite honestly, I think that is most boy's dream who were raised in the inner city. Well, by the time high school graduation rolled around, I realized those chances were about as slim as me. And if you know me, you know how slim I am. So, I guess professional baller isn't part of God's purpose for me, huh? Good news is it didn't take long after that for God to speak to me and let me know what's next for me. I got a call from my cousin in California to come out and visit for the holidays. The minute I landed, I knew that this is where I needed to be! I never knew what or how I would impact the world. Honestly, I'm not sure if anyone that has made an impact on the world really knew they were going to do it. They just knew they had to follow their heart.

So, I decided I was going to pack up and move to LA to try my luck in the entertainment industry. Now, mind you, I gave my life to God when I was young. I believe in the Lord and I would go to church when I could, but I know I've tip-toed on the line of what I can get away with in God's eyes. I know we all do some things in the heat of the moment where we have to stop and ask ourselves, "Is *this crossing the line?*" We may also say to ourselves, *"I just want to have fun, or I gotta do what I gotta do to survive."* I know we like to see what sins we can get away with before it eats our soul up completely. Well, Hollywood will push you to the limits with every soul test. And I was going to learn about it first-hand. The parties, the drinking, the drugs, and the women. For me, drugs were never an issue, growing up seeing my father addicted to crack pushed me far away from ever wanting to touch any drug. But, I did fall victim to alcohol and a love for women. I wouldn't say I was addicted to women, but now that I've taken counseling, I realized I had a void from my father not being around much that was filled by the attention of women. Fortunately, God has allowed me to stay on the straight and narrow path for my life up until this point. But the majority of my life, I've always had an issue staying committed in a relationship and letting my lack of discipline stunt my growth as a man. I was never taught commitment in a relationship. I came up in a single parent household. I watched my mother be in and out of relationships. Some relationships were more unstable than others. My father wasn't around much due to the drug addiction. All my boys had no fathers around either. As I got older, all I learned was the more girls you have, the cooler you are, or the more you are a man. When I did get to hang with my dad, it wasn't always the best situation for a kid. And as I got older my father would always ask about the girls I had. If I had any <u>girlfriends</u>, plural. Maybe subconsciously, that sent me on a mission to be with different women while searching for his approval.

On my journey for success I've been a hard worker, but could never really discipline myself 100% all the time. And as I got older, I've learned that most - if not all - men, that discipline starts with controlling our urge for women. I've had 3 long-term relationships and haven't been faithful in any of them. My first 2 didn't end due to infidelity, but they surely didn't stay strong because of it. The last relationship did however end from infidelity. And as crazy as it sounds, it was the biggest blessing in my life. Not saying it was a blessing to lose the woman of my dreams, but to wake up and realize right in time to turn my life around, man up, and take the necessary steps to do what I have to do to learn what it really is to become a man. To teach other men that you can be faithful. You can be disciplined. You can be face-to-face with temptation and come out on top. When you choose that path, not only will you stop hurting the people that mean the most to you, but e else in life will flow better. All of your blessings will flourish. You will be able to put all of your energy into what you really want out of it, and not let women distract you. In this book, I will let you in on my life and how I got to where I am today, and share my insights on what it takes to be a REAL MAN.

CHAPTER ONE

IT'S AT THE ROOT

IT'S AT THE ROOT

For you to understand the way you are as an adult, you have to dig deep into the past. Not only *your* childhood and upbringing, but your parent's childhood, upbringing, and even what occurred during their adulthood years. It is not only our physical features that go back generations, it is also our characteristics, mannerisms, and even habits. We as humans are not only programmed genetically, but also environmentally. Not only do we get similar looks passed down from our parents, grandparents, and ancestors, but our subconscious minds are very much programmed to run the same course as well. Which is why oftentimes addiction runs through generations of families. You may or may not have heard the term "generational curse" before. Abuse may run through generations of families. Also, infidelity, stealing, and poverty, could run through generations of families. On the positive side, you see hard working traits through generations who understand the importance of saving, healthy marriages, faithfulness, proper parenting, etc. Ultimately, it is up to each generation to break as many of the so-called, "generational curses" as much as possible and maintain the positive traits.

The only thing is, we are not taught how to do that or even taught that it is possible to do. We are just programmed from birth to carry on as our predecessors did.. It is said that our infant years, from birth to age 3, are the most important years for learning. Which is why a child can come into a multilingual family and grow up speaking multiple languages. Even though we don't think someone is affected by what they witness in their infant years, it is actually starting them off on whatever path of life you choose. As we get older, we are still not taught to break any of these subconscious programs. We watch our parent's tendencies, we mimic things we see on TV, we follow what our friends do...list goes on. The sad part is that the only way to gain knowledge on the issue is through reading books. And this is something we have to find out on our own. There is a quote that reads, "If you want to hide something from black people, put it in a book."

We usually don't go searching for these types of answers until something drastic happens in our life that forces us to go searching. I feel like it should be mandatory to learn about these things in school. While we learn about the history of our country, we need to learn the history of our own self. Get an early grip on the things we have been programmed to learn, and what we can do to shift the paradigm early to save the outcome of our future. We as young men need to be taught the importance of faithfulness and how this one disciplined act can set the tone for discipline in every other area of our lives. We need to be taught that we can break the unhealthy patterns that were passed down from our parents, and start a new way of being. I know there are a lot of things that could be changed in the school systems and in adolescence training - that is a whole other book in itself. But, from what I've witnessed as a man growing up, if you can get disciplined with sexual desires, you can become unstoppable in everything else.

Before I dive into my life, I want to back-track a bit, and give you a partial look into my parent's lives. Just to give you a better understanding of my Genetic and Environmental paradigm.

My mother, Joyce Anne, was born in Colorado on October 16, 1959. Unfortunately, her negative paradigm was set from the moment she was born. Her mother died giving birth to her due to complications. This left her father alone to grieve the loss of his wife, and be forced to take care of a newborn child, along with 3 other siblings. Luckily, my grandfather had his mother to help take care of her along, in addition to the help of his late wife's mother. The love from these two women during her infant years embedded the compassion and genuine love that my mother still carries within her until this day. Around age 5, her father remarried to a woman that was emotionally and mentally unstable. She convinced my grandfather to move the family to Minnesota, leaving the support of his mother behind. Therefore, my grandfather had to rely solely on his new wife to take care of my mom. Not long after settling into Minnesota, she started controlling my grandfather and separating him from his own children. She would only let him pay attention to her kids, and if he stood up for his own kid's, she would start to verbally abuse him. Tragic. Once she gained control over my grandfather, she then gained control over my mother and her siblings. The control started turning into verbal and physical abuse. Her father wasn't allowed to show her any love or affection - just sit back and witness the abuse take place. My mother dealt with this until she turned 18 years old, and decided to leave home to live with her sister and boyfriend on the military base in a small town outside of Chicago, Illinois. Not long after moving, she ended up meeting a guy she liked and moved to Chicago with him. This was not only her first relationship, but the start of being in abusive relationships. He started putting his hands on her and threatening to kill her. So, one day when he went to work, she packed all of her belongings and went to stay with a girlfriend that lived in the city. During this time, my mom met my father. He was an attractive, hard-working, aspiring actor and fashion model that seemed to have it all together on the outside, but on the inside was just as broken as her.

Oftentimes, more than not, it seems broken people are more inclined to finding each other. It's seems like they subconsciously attract each other, without putting forth much effort. My Father was born on the Southside of Chicago into an unhealthy paradigm of drug addiction. Both his mother and father were addicted to heroin and crack. Throughout my father's childhood, growing up on the Southside of Chicago, he witnessed it all - the drugs, the crime, the violence. His parents split up during his teenage years leaving him to live with his mother and her new boyfriend. After the split, my grandfather stopped coming around and pretty much abandoned my father. My father's stepdad started abusing him, while also allowing someone in the family to molest him. My father turned to the streets of Chicago for his outlet from what he was dealing with at home. He joined the Gangster Disciples Gang, started selling drugs, and eventually started using them. My father ended up graduating high school and going to college to follow his dreams in acting. He was actually one of the first people in our family to make it to college. However, he couldn't fully maximize his potential, because he couldn't shake his paradigm of the pain and unhealthy habits he had learned in his younger life. When my father met my mother, he had a job working at Amtrak and was trying to pursue his acting career, but little did my mom know to what extent his drug addiction was.

Eventually, my mother moved in with my father on the Southside of Chicago. My mom was one of the only white women on that side of town in the 80's, and based on some of the things my mom said they went through, its honestly a blessing that they made it out alive! Three years into their relationship, I was born May 5, 1987 at 5:55am at the Cook County Hospital. After three years of my parents trying to raise me on the Southside, dealing with my father's drug addiction, the criminal acts going on around them, and unstable family issues, my mother decided she didn't want to raise me there any longer. She wanted us to move to Minnesota to be closer to her family and away from the madness they were consumed in. About two years after the move, and my father started messing around on my mother with a woman he met at rehab. He ended up leaving me and my mother to be with this woman. My father was continuing the same lifestyle pattern he learned from his childhood. Addiction, abandonment, and self-hatred. I can't say it was intentional because my father loved me very much, but my father was broken and had no idea how to fix it, so instead he chose to run and let his addictions win. After he left, it was me and my mom on our own for the most part, until I graduated high school.

During the younger years I didn't understand why my father left us and what internal struggles he was dealing with. All I knew is I wanted to spend as much time with him as possible. My mother told me I used to sleep on my dad's chest every night when I was a baby, so I had that special bond with him from birth. When he left, my mother still wanted to allow him the ability to see me when he was in the right state of mind. I appreciate my mother for doing this for me, even though the situation led to a lot of disappointment for me. Because of his drug addiction, he did a lot of flaking on me and we wouldn't hear from him for weeks at a time. This never broke my love for him, but actually made me feel a deeper need for his love and attention. I wanted to understand how someone can claim they love you so much, but continue to hurt you and let you down time after time. I was too young to comprehend that it had <u>nothing</u> to do with me and everything to do with the battle he was fighting within himself. There were times he would pick me up to spend the weekend with him, and sometimes I could tell he was high. A couple times, he would even have random girls over getting high with him. I didn't want to let my mom know because I was scared she wouldn't let me go back.

As I got older and the pattern continued, he would spend some months in and out of prison, he would go on some good streaks of staying clean, and I would be able to spend more time with him – then, he would relapse and start back from the beginning. No matter what happened, my mother was always there to be lift me back up and explain to me that he wasn't doing this on purpose, and that my father was just sick, and we have to continue to love him and pray for him. She never spoke badly about him or tried to turn me against him. She always supported my love for him and would let him come around when he was back on his feet. Through all of this, it never made me hate him. It just increased my hunger and need for his attention. As I got older, I accepted the terms of our relationship, so I turned to sports in hopes of getting his approval. But, I would just end up getting more disappointment when he wouldn't show up for any of my games. I think he may have only come to two basketball games during my high school years. It hurt me because I felt hopeless, like there was nothing I could do. I had a mother who loved me with all her heart and did everything in her power to make sure we were good. The only issue was my mother was still broken herself, and left even more broken from my father. So, now she is in and out of abusive, unhealthy relationships. I remember when I was maybe seven or eight years old, her boyfriend at the time was yelling at her, and all of a sudden punched her so hard in the side of her head and burst her eardrum! I just remember running and jumping on his back trying to get him away from her. Then, first thing that came to mind was to call my dad to help. My first instinct with most of the things in my life were always to go to my dad. Her next relationship after that one seemed a little better to me, because I didn't see my mom get abused, but it was honestly no better than past relationships. The guy was a low-life that was still pulling my mom down. Luckily, witnessing the struggles my mother went through with men, I assured myself I could <u>never</u> put my hands on a woman. But on the downside, I never really learned the proper way to treat a woman. Not from my mother's situation and *surely* not from my father's situation.

I feel like there is no telling which direction a child is going to head. You hear stories about kids who come up in abusive households and follow the same path. Like my father, he followed the same path of addiction. I decided that I didn't want to follow the same path I witnessed growing up. I wanted to break the chain of addiction. My parents both struggled financially, I wanted to break that chain. I decided I wanted to take all the things I witnessed and do the complete opposite. Only thing is, I didn't go about it the right way. I took everything I went through and I bottled it up. I didn't talk to anyone about how I felt. I didn't seek counseling or guidance. I had no real male figure in my life to teach me the steps to be a man. In the midst of all that, I thought just because I didn't use drugs or get into trouble, I was doing the right thing. I didn't realize I was suppressing my pain. I didn't realize I was starting to search for something to fill the void my father left behind. The attention I was searching for in him. The acceptance I was searching for in him. I didn't realize I would start looking to fill that void with the attention of women

Have you ever sat and taken a look at your family patterns? What did you find?

_____

_____

_____

_____

What do you feel you have in common with your parents?

_____

_____

_____

_____

Do you believe in a generational curse? What do you think is yours? What have you done to change it?

_____

_____

_____

_____

_____

CHAPTER TWO

YOU'RE THE FRUIT

YOU'RE THE FRUIT

There's a saying that goes "The apple doesn't fall far from the tree" meaning a child usually has similar characteristics or similar qualities to his or her parents. Rather its life choices or life goals, in most cases, a child tends to follow suit of one or both parents combined. On the other hand, there are a group of children who tend to head towards going in the opposite direction. The determining factors can be subtle or major. Maybe it's in the genes, maybe the child wants to follow in the footsteps of a parent who was a professional athlete, maybe the parents were abusive, and the child thought this is the only way things are supposed to be. In my case, I decided I wanted to break the chain of poverty and addiction. I witnessed my mother fall victim to abuse, and I vowed I would never put my hands on a woman. I didn't understand as a kid why a man could do that. I looked at my mother as such a gentle kind loving person. Who would ever want to even come close to hurting her? Looking back on it now, I think I was so focused on making sure I never hurt a woman physically, that I didn't think about how easy it is to break a woman down in other ways.

The damage from being cheated on can actually in a lot of ways be worse than physical abuse. Not justifying abuse at all, but physical pain is instant. Wounds heal. Bruises eventually subside. A woman can look at the situation and asses it differently. When a man claims to love a woman and give his all to her, and then goes behind her back to give himself to another woman (or other women - plural) it completely breaks her down in so many ways. She's lost, confused, and broken. She wonders, "Is it my appearance? Was I not good enough? Did I push him away?" The pain from being cheated on can last forever. The images never go away. They stay embedded in a woman's mind, and play on repeat over and over. I was so focused on not laying my hands on a woman that I didn't realize that the deeper issues that I bottled up inside would lead me down a path of still emotionally hurting women. I didn't realize the path I was on.

I lost my virginity at age 16 in a rather unhealthy way. I was hanging out with my older cousin one day, and he had a girl over with him. I looked up to my cousin like the big brother I never had. I always wanted to do what he did, and I always found myself doing things to impress him. Since my father was never around, I guess he kind of filled the void of that male influential figure in my life. Anyway, back to the story…he had a girl over with us and were sitting on the couch watching TV. All of a sudden, out of the blue, he asked her to perform oral sex on me. She didn't hesitate at all, and came over to me and starred feeling on me. I didn't want him to know I've never done any of this before, so I went with it. While she was performing oral, he started having sex with her, and then handed me a condom and had me switch positions with him. Not trying to get too graphic, but I pretty much lost my virginity in a threesome. This was my introduction to what is supposed to be a beautiful bond between two people that love each other and are emotionally tied to each other. Your first sexual experience is supposed to be something a father sits his son down and explains to him how it should go. My first impression of sex set the tone for the rest of my teenage years, and adulthood. I didn't connect sex with love. I felt a sort of high from the situation. I felt accepted by the girl liking me enough to give herself to me. I will get into it later when I talk about seeking the right help to get to the core of my issues, but I learned that a lot of my problems stemmed from the abandonment my father left me throughout my childhood.

Luckily, I didn't get into too much trouble as a kid. Aside from my father's addiction, going to visit him in prison while he was locked up spooked me. One of the good things about my father is that he always gave great advice, even though he never followed it. He would always tell me never to follow in his footsteps. And he always told me I had way better things planned for my life and a jail cell is no place for anyone. So, I took that all in and made sure to keep myself away from trouble.

My early teenage years was the start of when I found myself at a lot of parties with my cousin. Since it was always with older kids, there was always a ton of drinking and smoking going on. I hated cigarettes because my mom smoked, and I hated the smell, so thank god I never picked up that habit. But, during this time, I started drinking. I really had no urge or a desire to drink, but I wanted to feel accepted and cool, so I started doing it as well. It's not that I was acting out, it was more so the fact that I didn't really have guidance. My mother gave me a lot of freedom as a kid. She was busy working and spending time with her boyfriends, so she would always tell me as long as I don't get in trouble with the law and keep my grades up, I can pretty much do as I please. I didn't really have a set curfew. If I wanted to miss a day of school, I could as long as my tardy marks didn't add up. So, again, I had no real reason to act out. I was a boy, so of course I found myself in some trouble every once in a while. Me and some friends used to ride around on our bikes throwing eggs at people. In the winter, we would hide on the 3rd floor of our apartment complex and throw water balloons at people. On occasion, we would steal from the local corner store to see what we can get away with. I think that's the biggest problem with boys - we want to see what and how much we can get away with.

As you become a man, that's one of the biggest issues that carry into adulthood –wanting to see how much we can get away with. A lot of men will lie until they actually get caught up in it. Most men cheat until they get caught, and are forced to change. Something about being a man and the mischievous nature that naturally run thru us. And with no real guidance and accountability, it can only get worse and more out of control the older you get. As long as my mom never caught me doing those things mentioned above, I thought it was ok. Now that I think about it, I may have learned this from my father. There was a lot of times I would be with my dad as a kid and if he was doing certain things, he would always tell me not to tell my mom. He would say, "She doesn't need to know everything." So, I carried that with me the rest of my life. Spending time with my dad when I did didn't really help me grow in knowledge of how to be a man, so when I was with my mom, the majority of the time I was just trying to figure everything out on my own. The older I got, life really became all about playing basketball, having fun, and getting girls. That's what everyone around me was doing. That's all my male friends and male figures talked about is sports and how many girls you can sleep with. Basketball was helping me keep my mind off of worrying about my dad and if he was ok, and when I would see him again. Getting attention and love from girls was boosting my ego and helped me feel special and accepted. It's weird how my mother's love and affection wasn't enough. I think I was so worried about getting the love from both parents and trying to understand what was going on with my father that it almost made me take my mom's love for granted. Looking back, she actually did more just to try to overcompensate, which is more than likely why I am such a loving compassionate person until this day.

I've always tried to hold myself accountable for my actions and assess who I am as a person, my view on life, what attributes I've attained from my parents, and if I have altered any for the better, or carried some of the same. I try to look back and see if I acted out at all during my adolescent years because of anything I witnessed while growing up. I try to look at why I surround myself around certain people. Why I felt the need to do certain things to be accepted. Why I felt the need to do certain things to impress other people, even if I knew deep down it wasn't truly me. Did this stem from my parents? Was I the apple that fell from the tree? Or did I change the course, but hold on to some things that still held me back from completely changing the paradigm?

I wanted to use work as a cover up for my pain. I would rather keep myself distracted than to think about the things that hurt me. I always wanted to be consumed with doing what I love to take my mind off of what was going on at home with my dad. It's amazing that I was blessed enough to have found a group of friends over the years that kept themselves out of trouble as well. We all had the same goals in life - to have fun and make money so we could do whatever we wanted and get whatever we wanted. Now see, my parents were both hustlers. During my entire childhood, my mother always worked two jobs to make sure we always had everything we needed. My father was a hustler as well, but my father really had to do whatever he could to survive. You can say my father was a product of his environment. Growing up in a household surrounded by drug dealers and thieves, naturally, not every hustle he did was right, but that's all he knew and you couldn't tell him differently. I definitely got their hustler's blood in me. I've been working since I was fifteen. Even before I was legally old enough to get a job, me and a buddy of mine used to stand on the corner in the city selling cans of soda for $1 each. I've been able to keep that hustler mentality with me 'til this day.

My father wanted to be an actor and model his entire life. He was booking some gigs in his 20's, but wasn't able to hold on to them due to drugs and his childhood nightmares haunting him and holding him back. I think that is another major factor that pushed me to be in the entertainment industry also. I wanted to carry on my father's dream and be successful at it for him. I guess it was another form of seeking his attention. But, in the midst of it I grew such a love for it all that I didn't even think about his acceptance - I wanted to do this to show *myself* I could do it. I also loved the spotlight. I found myself being the class clown in school. I loved the attention I got from the girls at my basketball games. And I knew that if I wasn't a professional athlete, the next best thing for attention would be an entertainer of some sort. So, why not shoot my shoot at everything? Acting, modeling, and music. I knew that if I could have succeeded, I could break generations of poverty, and I could get the attention and acceptance I thought I wanted or needed. Little did I know, when you are broken and dealing with some issues on the inside, no amount of attention and success can help you heal. It can only make the problem worse. You must get to the root of the problem and get real help. I will go into more detail about what I have done to heal in the chapter 'Get Help.' I am just thankful I realized I needed to get a hold on it before it was too late. A lot of times it takes losing the person you love, losing a job, or to the extreme of landing you in prison. As a man, I strongly encourage you to never let your ego or pride stop you from doing what you must do to reach MANHOOD and overcome your demons. We as men must learn that no matter what you did as a child in response to the issues you went through, you can always overcome and come out on top!

Looking back at your life do you think you acted out at all? If so, what do you think was the reason?

_____

_____

_____

_____

Did you learn any bad habits that you haven't been able to break? If you did how did you do it?

_____

_____

_____

_____

What will you do differently to ensure your children or future children become the fruit of a healthy tree?

_____

_____

_____

_____

CHAPTER THREE

HURT PEOPLE HURT PEOPLE

HURT PEOPLE HURT PEOPLE

There are only a few things in life that are certain. We all eventually die, and we all deal with pain. One of the worst forms of pain is being hurt by the people we love the most. The very people we put our trust into, and allow ourselves to be vulnerable with can have the power to hurt us deeply. The pain caused by someone we love can carry on for a lifetime and leave wounds that may never heal. It can make us put our guard up and lose trust in all of humanity. Rather its pain caused from a parent intentionally, such as physical abuse or verbal abuse, or unintentionally, such as neglect, lack of affection, or abandonment. The same can go for relationships. When we enter into a relationship with someone, we are giving them our all, we are trusting them with our happiness and our hearts. And if they hurt us, it can send our entire life spiraling out of control with no hope of return. The sad thing is most people enter into relationships broken, looking for someone to make them whole. Instead, it is our responsibility to become whole on our own. This is something I had to learn recently. I never witnessed many healthy relationships growing up, so I had no idea how to have one of my own. My whole life, I just did what I thought was right. I thought as long as you love someone to death that is all that matters. But, the fact is you must first love yourself to the point where you are willing to become whole. Until you do this, you can never really love someone the right way. You are bound to hurt them and let the pain you were caused project onto to them in an unhealthy way.

My mother's childhood of abuse and neglect left her searching for acceptance in a relationship and the feeling of never being good enough. It allowed men to take advantage of her and be abusive to her knowing she would allow it because she didn't know her worth. Fortunately, mother was able to eventually break free from the toxic situations and work on loving herself. My father followed suit with abandonment, since his father left him and really had nothing to do with him until he was an adult. My dad didn't downright *abandon* me, but I came second to his drug addiction, and by doing that, he projected the same pain onto me that his father did to him. The perfect example of a generational curse. My father believed in God and he would speak so much love and life into other people, but he was never able to implement it into his own life. He wasn't able to ever really love himself. It wasn't until I graduated and moved away from home that me and my father were ever really able to get close and develop the bond I was searching for with him.

I was never really one to dwell on the bad situations I faced in my life. I always tried to focus on my blessings and understand that there were people in the world dealing with way worse things than me. I would try to tell myself that the pain my father caused me wasn't *that* bad, so I would bottle the feelings up and carry on with my life. But, by doing that I let the pain inside me grow over the years and it subconsciously placed a limit on the way I could love. It allowed space for me to hurt people I love, specifically the women in my life.

I was in three serious relationships throughout the span of my life. The first one was two years, the second one was six and a half years, and my last one was about five years. I wasn't faithful in any of them. There is no excuse for cheating, and it's sad that the majority of men will cheat until they really understand what they must do to overcome it. I just finished reading Devon Franklin's book, 'The Truth About Men' and, man how I wish I had come up on this book fifteen years ago! The sad truth is even if I did, I don't think I would have been ready to follow it. Devon talks about how every man has a dog inside of them and how we must learn to tame it in order to really live a purpose-driven life. We must gain control of that wild dog on the loose hunting to please his hunger for temptation, and his disobedience that must learn to be controlled. You must learn how to make it obedient and disciplined. Get to the root of what is driving that wild dog, and gain control so you can be in charge of your temptations. I wasn't taught to be faithful by any men in my life. My father never encouraged it, none of my boys really encouraged it either. I never witnessed anyone around me in committed relationships, and the ones I did were messing around on the side. I wasn't stupid, I knew cheating was wrong and that I shouldn't do it, but I didn't really understand the effects it could have on a woman. I was always told by the men in my life you can mess around every once in a while, as long as you don't get caught, it won't hurt anyone. Horrible advice from other broken men that didn't know any better and have also followed a damaged paradigm. See, all I knew was to chase a woman, get her to fall for you, and sleep with her. It was some sort of thrill in it, and also some sort of fulfilment in it. When a girl decided to give herself to me, it was feeling that void of acceptance I was missing. It was a high I would get, and not even realize it. The pat on the back I got from my boys after sharing stories made me feel like I was doing the right thing. I thought I was showing how much of a man I was by how many women I could get. To me, it was a badge of honor. I was lost and confused.

My first relationship was puppy love, I was eighteen years old, and had just moved to California to be with a girl I met while I was on vacation in LA. I was not in any way ready to be in a relationship, but I was caught up in the moment, so I went for it. I was fresh out of high school and still trying to find my way. I was broke and relying on this girl for pretty much everything, both financial support and emotional support. She was the only person I knew in LA, other than my cousin. Because I had nothing going for myself, my confidence as a man was pretty low. I had no real direction in life. All I knew was that I wanted to be an actor and a rapper. I sat around her house all day waiting on her to come home while I was trying to figure out a way to make money, so I could take acting classes and get in the studio. It was honestly a very strange situation, now that I am looking back at it. My life pretty much revolved around her.

I would go back to Minnesota every few months to visit my friends and family. When I got home, I felt like I was breaking free from some sort of lockdown. I would shift into a single man mentality - not even thinking twice about my relationship back home. I was thriving off the freedom of being out with my boys and talking to other girls. I fell right into line with what everyone else was doing. I ended up cheating on her a couple of times on those trips, and I would feel horrible after doing it. The guilt would eat me up every time I got back home. I would ask God for forgiveness and strength to keep it from happening again, but the problem was I never asked God to help me. I never really thought to take <u>real</u> action. I never fully gave my life to God. I would fall right back into the same patterns.

The relationship didn't end from infidelity, we eventually ended up separating because I felt like she was trying to control me, and we would argue a lot because of it. She never found out about the cheating, but a woman's intuition is very strong, and I am sure she knew something was going on, which could have led her to the need to try and control our relationship. Even if she didn't know anything for a fact, I was still hurting her and hurting our relationship. After we split up, I was single for about a year before I got into another relationship. Throughout my year of being single, nothing healthy took place for my growth. I met some friends on the set of a movie while we were doing background work and ended up moving in with them after the break-up. It was an apartment of four, twenty-year-old boys full of testosterone, ready to take on LA and everything that came with it. All we were worried about was drinking and finding a new girl to hook up with. We would go to church every once in a while, but again like I said, we were definitely tip-toing with God just to see what we could get away with. We weren't even close to submitting our lives to live the right way.

After about a year of all of us being single, one of my boys ended up dating a girl and brought me over to her house to introduce me to her friend. We hit it off right away. We were both into music and got to drinking wine and talking about music all night. I ended up staying at her house all week. The thing about me is when I love, I love **hard**.

If I like you, I want to be around you all the time. What was supposed to be one night of fun turned into a six-and-a-half year relationship. It flowed super easy early on. The chemistry was there. We wanted to be with each other 24/7. I had no desire to be with any other woman. I thought she was the one I was going to be with for the rest of my life. I proposed to her about six months into the relationship. I knew nothing about marriage or what it looked like, but I was head over heels for her.

After the honeymoon phase wore off and the real tests came rolling in, I didn't know how to stand strong. I slowly started to fall back to my old ways. I let the dog in me come out. I wanted to be out with my boys all night. I felt like the more she tried to hold on to me, the more I would push her away. I thought I knew how to love her the right way, but really, I had no idea. I would be entertaining girls on different dating sites. Me and my boys would be hanging out with other girls all night. I was breaking her heart day-by-day, and didn't even realize what I was doing. I really thought this was normal behavior for a man. I was following all of the things I witnessed my whole life. I was searching for pointless attention and rebelling for no reason. I was following the same steps my father did to me by hurting the person I claimed to love. By the time it came to the end run of our relationship, the trust was so damaged, we were holding on simply because of the comfort of being together for so long.

The last year of our relationship was when I went on America's Next Top Model, I had to live in a house with other models for almost two months. When I came home from filming, things got so much worse. It's not that I changed as a person, or let the fame from the show get to my head. It was the fact that the fame brought a new level of attention for women, and a new urge for me to be free to explore. I was lost and had no grasp on the right way to take on my career, newfound fame, and be the right man for my girl. I was immature and unwilling to do what I needed to do to man up for my relationship. Instead, I drug her along this crash course while I went on the road every week hosting at night clubs, performing, and partying. I would leave her home all night to wonder what I was doing. I started partying more when I would get back home from being on the road. If she would question me, I would feel like she wasn't respecting me as a man, and it would lead to another argument. There were times when I was unfaithful and she never found out, but again a female's intuition is strong – so I knew she knew *something*. It ate her up inside not knowing what was really going on, driving herself crazy wondering if I was messing around on her or not. I was sick and didn't even realize it. I knew it wasn't right and that I shouldn't be doing it, but again I would make excuses that every man cheats, and that as long as I love her while I am with her it will make up for it. The men around me encouraged the behavior because that is all they knew as well. The applause from other guys and celebrities around me boosting my ego only fed the beast more. This went on for about a year before we finally realized this wasn't healthy for either of us, that we were going to end up eventually resenting each other. Regardless of if we were falling out of love with each other, we still had enough love for each other to know it was time to walk away. No matter how many good times you can have with someone, if one person is broken, there is something deep they must work on in order to really make a relationship last forever. I think she knew that I was broken inside, she realized that there was no way this could ever work with me hurting her over and over again with no signs of hope for me changing anytime soon.

After we split up, I continued my crash course with women full speed ahead. While my career was rising and my fame was growing, my actions for growth in life were really declining. At this point, I was <u>rarely</u> going to church, my only focus was hanging out with my boys, partying, and meeting new women. The majority of my work only fed all of this behavior. I would do my photoshoots during the day, and my nights and weekends would be all about getting drunk with the boys and hooking up with girls. It's crazy how people say, "Well, boys will be boys", or "This is just a phase of life men have to go through." But it's really not. There are much healthier phases of life men should be going thru. Mind you, I would never want to change anything in my life because my journey has brought me here to tell my story and hopefully, help some men get on the right course - but trust me when I say, the path of a man's life should not just consist of getting drunk and hooking up with girls. How many tequila shots you can take or how many girls you can sleep with does not make you a man. The discipline to know that you **can** sleep with a woman and choose **not** to is what makes you a real man. I see that clearly now, since I am closer to God. There has to be some guidance to teach men the right way. I didn't have it, so I figured it out the hard way. They say it often takes something dramatic to happen to someone for them to change their ways. The death of a loved one, a near-death experience, a spouse or significant other leaving, can all spark change within someone. For me, it took losing the love of my life to finally wake up and understand this isn't the way to live. To get to the bottom of my issue, to fully submit to God, and commit to changing my mindset.

My last relationship went from being a three-year friendship to an almost five-year relationship and engagement. Liane and I were friends for two years with no initial intention of ever dating. We were both in relationships with other people and never came close to crossing the line. It just so happened that both of our relationships ended around the same time, so we were kind of each other's shoulder to lean on. I was single for a little over a year after the break-up, and throughout that time, me and Liane would hang out on a consistent basis. Then, we'd go months without seeing each other. When we were together, we had a natural connection with each other - it flowed. I enjoyed her company. She was beautiful with a good sense of humor. She wasn't full of herself. She was family-orientated and believed in God. We hit it off without any effort. I loved everything about her as a person. Another rare thing about her was that her name wasn't tarnished in Hollywood. She didn't have a reputation for sleeping around with guys. That is rare to find in the Hollywood scene. She was someone I could see myself being with, but I was not ready to be in another relationship at the moment. I was caught in this young, wild, and free phase. All I was interested in was running the streets with my boys, and being on the road three days out of the week hosting at clubs. As crazy as it sounds, no matter where I was in the world, or what I was doing, I would always think about Liane.

Around Halloween 2014, we randomly connected with a group of friends to go to a haunted hayride. This was the time I really felt something different regarding Liane. I wanted us to be more than just friends. I thought I was ready to take things to the next level. A lot of people warned her about me, told her how I was a cheater in my past relationship, and how I've been around in Hollywood. They told her I was going to break her heart and she needs to run as far away from me as possible in the other direction. She saw more in more though. Our connection was too strong, and she was willing to risk it all. I thought I was going to be able to change my ways for her, but I was broken and hadn't done anything to fix it. No matter how much I gave her love, affection, and gifts to overcompensate the fact that I couldn't let go of the hunger for other women's attention, it didn't make up for it one bit. I still ended up letting her down. I still ended up breaking her heart. I still ended up proving those people right.

You may ask how can a man cheat on someone they claim to love? How can they cheat on a woman that does everything for them? Beautiful, loyal, good sex, one who builds with them career-wise. The thing is, a man cheating doesn't have anything at all to do with the love of his woman. A man could be willing to take a bullet for his girl, but if he doesn't have control of that dog inside of him, he will still run astray and come right back. For men, sex and love are separate. Women equate sex with emotions, while men do not. We can sleep with a girl and never think twice about her again. It is a sad truth, but there is no connection between the two. That is why we can love our women with all our heart, and still be on the search for other physical satisfaction. It is the main reason you as a man must learn to train your mind. You must learn to set boundaries so you can never get yourself in a similar situation. Set boundaries with other women, boundaries with drinking, going to night clubs, and watching pornography. Whatever it is that can leave you vulnerable to the dog inside breaking free, set boundaries. Liane would always warn me about this, but I was too stubborn to listen. I thought I was strong enough to control myself in any situation, but I was really as weak as they come.

The last situation was the end of the rope for us. We had just gotten engaged in August 2019, and even though I knew she was the girl I wanted to spend the rest of my life with, I was not mentally or spiritually ready for marriage. I had a female friend that I used to hook-up with before Liane and I got together. I never told Liane about anything that ever happened between us, I just told her that she was always only a friend. This was the first mistake. When you enter into a relationship, you need to cut ties with anyone you have ever slept with. There is really no reason for a man to have female friends while in a relationship, especially any he has previously slept with. If you don't have kids with another woman, there is really no need for you to keep in touch with her. This is something I should have known, but again the brokenness inside of me for whatever reason thought it was ok. Maybe in my subconscious, I was hoping we could do something sexual again. Well, it ended up being tested. We would talk off-and-on throughout the relationship. A few months after the engagement, we were texting each other and got on the subject of one of our old hook-ups. One thing led to another and we even took it as far as talking about doing it one last time before I became a married man. How could I be doing this behind the back of a woman that I love with all my heart and plan on spending the rest of my life with? Even worse with a woman I have her hanging out with? How sick could I be? The answer is very sick. No woman deserves any of it. I knew it was wrong right after the conversation was over. I felt like I was losing control of myself. I said a prayer asking God to forgive me and help me be right for Liane.

God answered my prayers. Not in a way I thought I wanted at the moment, but in a way he knew it had to happen. Liane ended up reading those messages in my Apple watch a month later. It ended our relationship immediately. As crazy as it sounds, I needed it to end. I needed to lose the love of my life to fully submit to God and turn my life around. This was the wake-up call I needed to pull my head out of my ass and change my mentality. To allow myself the ability to dig deep and find out what it really means to be a Man. There is no way we could have entered into a marriage with me being in the broken state I was in. I didn't want it to end - I was planning on getting married to her, and now she hated me and wanted nothing to do with me. I was losing my mind trying to do everything in my power to get her back. I was trying to force her to give me another chance and take me back. I wasn't able to look at the bigger picture that God was trying to paint, what he was trying do for me. I was so desperate trying to hold on to her and not let go that I didn't realize immediately that this had to happen in order for God to wake me up and work on me. I had to let her go and get my life together. As strange as it sounds, the curse of me breaking her heart ended up being my biggest blessing to date. It kills me that she had to be the one to go thru it for me to figure it out. But she is one of the strongest women I know. And if God needed to put any woman in my life to be strong enough to endure it, it is Liane. This was what I needed for me to really find my purpose. To help other hurt men break the chain of hurting women. I'm not justifying what happen or saying that it's ok, given the circumstance. It's not fair that Liane or any of the other women in my life had to deal with what I put them through, but I accept my path from God. I can't change my past, but I can secure my future. I want to be living proof that men can change. Men don't have to entertain multiple women. Men don't have to sleep around with a ton of women to be cool. That's the young immature way of thinking. Men can stop cheating and reverse the pattern. We can put the right amount of work in and train our minds to only be focused on our Queen. I will go into more depth about what I did to help me change my mindset in the chapter 'Make a Change.'

Me and Liane are still not together at the moment and I'm not sure what God has in store for us. I feel like our purpose together can be bigger than our purpose apart. I feel like we have something bigger to do together to show the world that love wins. So, I will leave it in God's hands and trust the process. If it is meant for us to come back together even stronger, it will be. Liane, if you're reading this, just know I'm a changed man, deserving of a second chance.

Why do you think it takes something dramatic to happen for a change to occur?

_____

_____

_____

_____

Why do you think it takes so long to want to change old ways?

_____

_____

_____

_____

Why do you think men feel a sense of accomplishment by getting with new women?

_____

_____

_____

_____

CHAPTER FOUR

FORGIVE

FORGIVE

"And whenever you stand praying, forgive, if you have anything against anyone,
so that your Father also who is in heaven may forgive you your trespasses."
Mark 11:25

"Christ Jesus came into the world to save sinners – of whom I am the worst.
But for that very reason I was shown mercy so that in me, the worst of sinners,
Christ Jesus might display his immense patience as an example for those who
would believe in him and receive eternal life."
Timothy 1:15-16

"Get rid of all bitterness, rage and anger, brawling and slander,
along with every form of malice. Be kind to one another, tenderhearted,
forgiving one another, as God in Christ forgave you."
Ephesians 4:31-32

In order to be forgiven you must first forgive yourself and the people that have hurt you in your life. Once you have forgiven yourself and those people, you can then repent and ask God for forgiveness. There is no greater weight that is lifted off of you than when you truly forgive yourself or someone who has hurt you. It is the key factor in being able to truly start any healing process in your life. To act in the true purpose of life, which is love, it is necessary to be a forgiving person no matter how bad the circumstances. It is easier said than done I know, but when you are able to accomplish it, an immediate sense of freedom is released. Forgiveness is truly for YOU, not the other person.

I was able to forgive my dad before he passed away almost three years ago. I got the chance talk with him and let him know the pain he caused me. I let him know I understood it wasn't intentional. I understood it was the drugs that took control of him. I let him know I was thankful for the time we were able to spend together and the bond we were still able to form over the years. At the point of forgiving him, I still didn't really understand the underlying issues it caused in my life. How the lifestyle I was living was deeply rooted to the emotions that I had bottled up over the years. The unconscious search for acceptance I was still seeking. This was something I learned more recently since seeking counseling, but I wanted him to know that I still loved him with all my heart. I wanted him to know I forgave him and that I wanted him to forgive himself.

Other than my father being addicted to drugs, he was a great man. He was a God-fearing, loving, selfless person who just couldn't shake the brokenness inside of him. He told me he forgave himself, though I'm not sure if he ever really could. I know for a fact my father was able to give his life to the Lord and repent for his sins before he passed. I lost my father due to his battle of addiction in 2016. He was clean for almost six months before his final relapse. He overdosed from a bad batch of cocaine mixed with Fentanyl. He wasn't able to overcome his addiction, but I know he asked the Lord for forgiveness before he passed away, because he would do it every night before he went to sleep. I believe deep down in my heart that my father was at peace when he died, and his soul was forgiven.

My entire life, I tried to make it a point to pride myself on my caring heart. I was always thoughtful and took other people's feelings into regard with my actions. I've also always been a man who took responsibility for my actions when I was wrong. My intentions were never to hurt any woman in my life. Unfortunately, I can't take back what I have done, but I can make it a point to forgive myself and never let it happen again. I can make it a point to try and help stop other men from making the same mistakes I have made in life. I can direct them to the things that helped me change.

Forgiveness is one of the main factors in change. It's is a major element in the growth process. Resentment can literally eat at you to the point of sickness. It will always be in your mind, holding you back from moving forward. You cannot let something go until you truly forgive.

We were put on earth to make mistakes and learn from them. You have to go thru periods of pain to understand your purpose. Life is too short. Once you realize all we are promised is the moment you are in, you can understand that holding on to a grudge is a complete waste of energy. Rather it's with yourself for bad choices you made throughout your life, or something horrible that someone did to you. Unforgiveness will not change any of the circumstances, it will only hinder you from making progress in the long run. Cleanse yourself of the negative energy as soon as possible, and let it go. A good way I've learned to forgive is knowing everything that happens is meant to happen. For whatever reason no matter how big or small it was meant to be. I don't believe God makes mistakes. So, if you can understand that then you can forgive easier. You can let the past remain in the past, and move on with creating the most positive future possible. The things you can't forgive yourself for, you have to bring to God and leave it with him. God is the only one that can judge us. He is the only one that can really hold anything over our heads. The things that other people have done to you, bring them to God. He will be the one that deals with everyone accordingly.

If you are going thru a situation that you are seeking forgiveness for, don't be afraid to talk to someone close to you, or seek counseling. I know forgiveness isn't always an easy task, but talking to a parent or close friend or family member can help put things into better perspective. Sometimes it helps to talk to someone outside our family like a psychiatrist or therapist that will not cast judgment on you, and that deals with personal issues on a daily basis. If you need to forgive yourself for something you may have done, or tend do repeatedly, it is best to write out a solid plan to overcome the problem(s). Any problem can be fixed - it just takes the right amount of work. Any addiction can be broken, any habit can be broken; it all depends on how badly you want to break it. Once you forgive yourself, then you put the excuses aside, and put the work in to make sure you never have to apologize for it again. If someone that you love is hurting you time after time, you have to first forgive them, then assess the situation. Just because you forgive them doesn't mean you have to continue to deal with them and allow them to keep hurting you. You may have to love them from afar while they work on themselves. They may need to lose you for a moment to really learn and grow, so they can never hurt you again. The first step to moving forward in life is forgiveness, regardless if the relationship between the two of you is salvageable or not.

CHAPTER FIVE

LETTER TO MY DAD

LETTER TO MY DAD

Dear Pops,

I forgive you for the hurt you caused me as a child. I forgive you for the hurt that stuck with me unconsciously throughout my adulthood. I know you didn't mean to hurt me and mom. I know you loved us to death and would have given your life for either one of us. I know you were fighting so much brokenness, that you were running from your own issues. I know you were never taught the right ways to be a father. You fell victim to an unhealthy paradigm and never properly shifted it. I forgive you for not showing me how to be the right type of man in a relationship, I understand that you were never taught that as well. You showed me love when you could and I'm beyond grateful for the time I did get with you. I know you wanted things to be different, you just didn't know how to fix it. I understand that everything happens how it is supposed to, the things we went thru helped me get to this point in my life. As I got older, we got closer and I'm thankful for that. I love the positive attributes I got from you, the hustler in me, my fearlessness, even my passions to follow in your footsteps as an actor. I'm thankful I got to spend my 30th birthday with you. You and mom made it a special one. I am at peace knowing that the last time I spoke to you, we were on good terms and I was able to tell you that I love you. I am at peace knowing that you were forgiven for your sins from our Lord and Savior, Jesus Christ when you passed away. I know we never got to have the relationship we both wanted our entire life, but I'm thankful for how close we were able to grow. I wish you were able to be here and watch me raise my children at some point, but I know you will be right here with me in spirit. I know this is not the end and we will be reunited again. Until that day comes, I want you to know I miss you, I forgive you, and I love you.

Sincerely,

Deuce

What are some things you need to forgive yourself for in order to grow in life?

_____

_____

_____

_____

Do you believe everything can be forgiven? If not, what is unforgiveable in your eyes?

_____

_____

_____

_____

Write your favorite Bible verses on forgiving, and look at them whenever you need the strength to forgive.

_____

_____

_____

_____

_____

CHAPTER SIX

MAKE A CHOICE

MAKE A CHOICE

I always wondered why you see some people turn their life around for the better, and some people stay the course of disaster until the day they die. What is the desire to become the best version of yourself? To decide that you want to do the right things in life, to stop making excuses, and make a choice to renew yourself? What makes someone wake up and realize that they are hurting the people they love on a daily basis? My father never figured it out. He wasn't able to overcome his addiction before he passed away. I wanted to break all negative paradigms passed down to me. I made a choice that I will not allow any negative stigmas to tarnish my destiny.

Everyone's breaking point is different. For me, it was losing the woman I wanted to spend the rest of my life with. It was seeing the pain I caused her, and our family forcing me to take a step back and realize that I was doing the same thing my father did to me and my mother. My entire life, I always told myself I would never bring pain to the people I love, and here I was doing it. I have no idea why it took so long to figure it out. I wish I could've been taught the right ways to become a man when I was young, but if that was so, I wouldn't be here telling this story. I needed it to happen at this moment in my life, so I could mentor and guide other young men.

Not only was I about to enter into a marriage as a broken man, my career was in a bit of limbo at the moment. I had been feeling stuck and unmotivated. After my father passed away, I had no urge to work. I left my modeling agency. I was sitting around waiting on opportunities to come to me. I was starting to see my confidence drop. Liane was always in high spirits, focused, and her work was flowing on the rise. I started to question myself as a man and where my life was heading. I started doubting my potential and losing faith of what God had in store for me. I was letting go of all the positive things I taught myself to get to this point in my life, such as increasing my faith in God, manifesting what I wanted out of life, etc. I was one foot in and one foot out with everything I was doing. I was worried about impressing other people and wanting to feel accepted. I was doing what I thought my boys would think was cool, doing what my peers thought was cool and doing things that society deemed "being a man." The image I thought I had to uphold as a rapper or model was causing me to lose myself, and I could feel it in my spirit. The situation involving breaking up with my ex freed me. I saw it as an opportunity to renew myself.

I wanted to give my life to God and start over. I wanted to do the work to change my mindset and the way I looked at everything in life. I wanted to figure out the real purpose of my life, and life in general. I wanted to let go of any image anyone can paint of me, and paint my own image of myself. I wanted to get to the bottom of why men cheat and how the men that stopped cheating overcame it. I needed to find out the deep-rooted issues I had going on inside me that caused me to do what I had done. What was it that made me tip-toe on the line of good and bad even when I knew what wasn't right? Why did I think the lifestyle I had been living was ok? Why did I make excuses for the things I had done? Why did I need to feel accepted from other men? Why did I need attention from women other than my Queen, just to feel special? Just because you are an attractive successful man does not mean you need to be for everyone. I haven't been around many men in my life that understood this. I needed to find the answers from the men that figured out how to live righteous. I was eager to put the past behind me and start this new journey.

The first thing I did to start my change was call my longtime pastor, Touré Roberts. I've been going to Pastor Touré's church for at least the past ten years. When I first started going to his church, I swear there was about 15 people at the service, including myself. Now, he has a church in the heart of Hollywood, and a location in Denver, Colorado. He is beyond anointed and was one of the first people I thought about when starting this journey. So, I called up PT and walked him through what happened with me and Liane. We talked for quite some time about what I did, if I forgave myself for it, and if I asked forgiveness from God. We talked about the lifestyle choices I had been making up until this point. I explained where my heart has been and how I wanted to give my life to God and start over.

I can't lie, I was broken losing my girl, but he put things into perspective for me with where this loss was going to take me as a man of God. He told me some stories about when he changed his life around, and finally gave his life to the Lord, when he made the commitment to be faithful in his relationships and in faith. He said a prayer for me asking God to forgive me for my sins and walk with me on this new journey. When he finished saying the prayer, I burst into tears. I felt the Holy Spirit come over me. I felt this complete feeling of freedom like my entire past had been wiped clean. My mind had never felt so clear in my entire life. I felt an immense amount of joy and happiness in my heart. I never wanted the feeling of clarity to end, I knew this was the true feeling I had been searching for my entire life. It sounds crazy but it's true, I finally understood my calling. After the prayer, he told me to read his book 'Wholeness,' so I ordered that along with a few other books that were referred by other men of faithfulness. The other books I ordered were:

- 'Wholeness' by Toure Roberts
- 'Every Young Man's Battle' by Stephen Arterburn and Fred Stoeker
- 'The Wait' by Devon Franklin and Meagan Good
- 'The Truth About Men' by Devon Franklin
- 'Redeemed Like David: How to Overcome Sexual Temptation' by Mark Ballenger
- 'Understanding and Overcoming Temptation' by Dr. Daniel Morris

- 'The Way of the Superior Man' by David Deida
- 'Think and Grow Rich' by Napoleon Hill
- 'You2' by Price Pritchett
- 'As A Man Thinketh' by James Allen

I recommend every last one of those books that I listed, not only for the men but for the women as well. I read all of those books in a three-month time span, and when I tell you my mind is completely renewed! They answered every question I was searching for, not only on why men do the things they do, but also how to reprogram your mind. 'Every Man's Battle' gives every man the knowledge and armor needed to fight any and all temptations. It lets women in on the way a man's mind works. 'The Truth About Men' also touches on the battle of temptation we as men have to overcome. Devon refers to it as a Dog inside of us that we must learn to tame and keep in control. 'Wholeness' speaks on self-love and becoming whole for yourself before you can truly love anyone else. Because I was also lost career and confidence wise, 'Think and Grow Rich' completely reprogrammed my mind back to a positive frequency. It helped me remember what I have manifested into my life thus far, and everything I can manifest once I get back on the right frequency.

I was blessed to have also been able to talk with Devon Franklin about my situation and steps I needed to take in order to grow into this new person. Devon is the perfect example for me to follow because he is also in the entertainment industry, so he knows the level of temptation that comes with it, and how to defeat it. Along with Devon, I was also able to get guidance from my producing partners Rhyan Lamarr and Bishop Eric D. Garnes, both men that have learned how to maneuver faithfully through the entertainment industry. When you are elevating to a higher level, surround yourself around people that are walking the path you are attempting to walk. Reach out to people you look up to. Social media and the Internet are both beautiful tools nowadays. Everyone can be contacted through sending a direct message. You would be surprised at the replies you could get back if you sent a question to some people in position to help. I try to reply to my followers as much as possible with advice I can give. There are even times when I reach out to celebrities on a larger platform than me, and get replies with advice. No disrespect to my friends or family, but in order for me to learn new things, I had to position myself around new people.

When me and Liane had some issues early in our relationship with cheating, I started talking to her life coach, Tony Gaskins. He was starting to take me down a good path to elevate my mind, but I wasn't ready at the moment, and lost touch with him. This time, I had to make it a point to stay under his wing. This time I was ready for his advice and hungry for the knowledge and wisdom. His story is also proof that men can change if they really want to. Tony is the reason I decided to take action and write my book. I wanted to write a book for a while, but didn't really know what it would be about and had no idea where to begin. The timing was finally perfect, and he was there to help guide me through the entire process. He told me I didn't need a ghostwriter, and that I can have the whole book finished within a month all by myself. His wisdom has helped my growth not only in faithfulness, but now as an author as well.

I've learned that when you are making the effort to take a step in the right direction, God will provide you with the help you need and put the right people in your life to assist you. When you make one step, God takes five more on your behalf. All of the men that have been placed in my life recently have all been like guardian angels in their own right. The wisdom and assistance they have provided me has set my process of growth light years ahead of what I ever could have imagined. I encourage all men to have a mentor of some sort that can help guide you - not only in your career, but also in your spiritual journey. It is good to find someone that has walked a similar path as you, and made it to the next level. Your mentorship may not even be a personal relationship. It may be someone you choose to study online or study their books. Regardless of what method you choose, the mentorship will be a key factor in your growth.

You cannot reach your full potential in life without some sort of connection to God. Whatever God you believe in you must have an understanding that there is a creator that put us here for a divine and specific reason. We were not just put on earth to move freely and do what we wish. We were put here to live in the image of God, to love and create. The more I learn and study, the more my yearning for knowledge grows. The more my spirit craves positive energy and healthy choices.

To grow to my ultimate potential, I had to cut out behaviors and habits that were catering to the old me, and replace them with new ones. I stopped drinking liquor completely - it takes me out of control and can allow for slip-ups. It's also horrible for your body and spirit. I think a glass of wine every now and then is fine, but for me I decided to stop drinking everything. I unfollowed all the females I know on Instagram that post revealing pictures. I stopped looking at the explore page on Instagram as well, if I do, I make it a point to swipe past any females. I stopped watching pornography. I used to think it was ok to watch it every now and again, but now that I am walking in purpose, I understand the dangers of it. I used to bring my phone with me every time I went to the bathroom. Now I will leave it and bring a book. This turns aimless browsing on social media into productive learning. It will also eliminate the option to look at pornography. If you do this, it will also be healthy for a relationship. Your girlfriend or wife won't have to worry about if you are sneaking around behind their back or up to something.

To stay productive, I set the daily timer on my Instagram to an hour a day. I do a lot of my work on social media, so setting the timer lets me get in and make whatever posts I need to, reply to some followers, and then get off the app without aimless browsing. I read for thirty minutes a day and meditate for 10-15 minutes a day. During the meditation, I visualize the positive things I want to acquire in my life, and all the things I am grateful for. I like to read self-help books rather than fiction. If I'm going to use my imagination, I want to put it towards building different areas of my career. When sex scenes come on TV, I will bounce my eyes away from the screen until it is over, so my mind doesn't start to wander. I had to train my eyes and my mind. I learned this in 'Every Man's Battle' you have to gain control of your eyes. I do this in public as well - if you are looking at a woman and you start to think sexual thoughts, you have to learn to bounce your eyes and switch your thoughts. What I tell myself when I catch my eyes wandering is, "I've made a covenant with my eyes and mind." It helps me understand the bigger picture of why I'm doing it and it helps stop temptation on site. Most men might say all these things are a bit much, it won't hurt to catch a glimpse of a random girl, or I can watch sex scenes in movies and look at half-naked girls on Instagram. But, if you are in a relationship, doing these things allows you to focus all of your sexual energy on your partner only. It will actually make your sex life better because your partner won't be getting parts of you, and you may not be subconsciously thinking about another girl. All of your energy will be on her. All of your sexual desires will be of your Queen. You will notice once you start doing this how much more needy you become for your partner's touch. If you are single, it will help you put your energy towards something productive, rather than wasted sexual daydreams, or the searching for your next hook-up. It will help you look at a woman beyond sexual thoughts and be more interested in the mental and spiritual connection. When you start dating someone new, they will be the only one you are focused on.

Music is a big influence in the world sexually as well. Since I am a rapper, I used to just say whatever sounded good. I would try to tell stories when I could, and always made it a point to never let my music get too dirty, but now I'm making sure my music is clean and positive only. It's honestly hard for me to listen to a lot of rap nowadays, so the transition has been pretty easy for me. Majority of rap lyrics are negative and talking about drugs or degrading women. I've been listening to a ton of gospel rap lately. Some dope artists I have in rotation are Bizzle, NF, Eshon Burgundy, Lecrae, Social Club Misfits, and 1K Phew, to name a few for you.

These have been key factors in reprogramming my brain to fight temptation and sexual thoughts. To reprogram my paradigm to positive frequencies, I also watch church online daily and Law of Attraction videos daily. If you can gain control of your mind, you will be undefeated. As far as church videos, I watch a lot of Rick Warren on YouTube, and

I study Bob Proctor regularly for Law of Attraction videos. Both are masters of their teaching and can change your entire outlook on life.

By making these changes, if I can encourage just <u>one</u> person around me to make some adjustments in their life, I have succeeded. I have passed the torch. Though, the goal is to touch *millions* with the changes that have been helping me. If you have felt some kind of motivation to grow from this, then please pass it along. Let's keep building our men into the soldiers the Lord put us here to become.

What are some things you need to change in your life in order to grow?

_____

_____

_____

_____

How long do you think it takes someone to change their behaviors? Do you think once they change, they can stay that way for good? If not, why?

_____

_____

_____

_____

What are the biggest influences in your life? Are they positive influences?

_____

_____

_____

_____

CHAPTER SEVEN

DEAR FUTURE WIFEY

DEAR FUTURE WIFE

Dear Wifey,

I wanted to write you a letter that you will be able to look at for the rest of your life and know how much I love you. A letter to look at and be reassured that those words hold true because they are coming from a man that put the work in to learn how and heal his brokenness. To understand what it takes to be a Real Man for his woman and himself. To stand behind those words one hundred percent. I now know what it means to step up and be a man in every category. In Faithfulness, in Romance, in Ambition, in Patience, in Communication, and in thoughtfulness. I know relationships are work, and I'm willing to put in however much work it takes to make it last an eternity.

I am also writing this letter for myself, so I can look back and be reminded of who I am, the vows I've made, and the responsibility I hold. You deserve the world and I am committed to making that a reality. I've done some things in my past that I'm not proud of, but the lessons I learned from them have helped shape me into the person I am today. I know a man's trust and loyalty is everything to his woman and I want you to be secure knowing I will do everything in my power to protect your trust in me and feel my loyalty.

I need a woman that is going to challenge me to always be the best version of myself, a woman that will allow me to challenge her to always be the best version of herself. I am thankful to know that we have found that in each other. I will be an amazing loving father to our children, and I will shower them with as much love as they need, but know when to whoop their butts when they need it too. Just kidding, but seriously I will make sure you get every bit of me every step of the way. I will help you raise them into amazing, loving adults. I will be the man that you and the kids need every day of my life.

I want to travel the world with you and see places we have never seen before.

I want you to be the first person I share good news with, and I want to be the first person to hear your good news. I want to rub your back and feet after a long day and remind you how wonderful tomorrow will be, regardless of the stress that today brought. I want to show you what it's like to fall completely in love with the man of your dreams and have no worries about what the future holds, other than what we are going to eat for dinner. I know we will have our disagreements and our arguments, but I want to end everyone with a kiss goodnight. We will never go to bed angry, because I know how short life is and there is no argument worth going to sleep mad about. I've learned the purpose of life is to live in the image of God. That is to do everything out of love. So, with that, love wins. I choose love.

Write a letter to your future wife or husband below:

_____

_____

_____

_____

_____

_____

_____

_____

_____

_____

_____

_____

_____

CHAPTER EIGHT

BE THE MAN YOU WISH RAISED YOU

BE THE MAN YOU WISH RAISED YOU

I always had an image in my head of how I wanted my dad to raise me as a kid. Even though most of my boys growing up didn't have their fathers in their lives either, I knew it was supposed to be different. I would always imagine having a childhood like I saw in the movies or on TV where both parents are together and happy, cheering in the stands at basketball games. Then, after the game they take the team out for pizza or burgers, and at night they tuck the kid in and read a bedtime story. I don't know if I really cared much about the bedtime story part, but I did want my parents together. I did want to look up in the stands at my basketball games and see my dad next to my mom cheering me on. I'm beyond thankful for everything my mother did to shower me with love and support, but at the end of the day a boy needs his dad around.

I don't have any kids at the moment, but I definitely want to get started in the near future. I would love to have a son to be able to do all the things for him I wish my dad did with me. I know we always want our sons to do the things we as men never did. Get them started in sports right away, get them the right training. Watch them grow up and become professional athletes. That sounds like the dream. But what if I have a girl? Will I still take the same steps to make sure she becomes a professional athlete? I don't think so. I think that's when mom comes in and tries to direct her down the path of where she sees her dreams going. Aligning their career goals are great and all, but it's deeper than all that honestly. For me, what's really important is that I want to be there for my kids. I want to be there to show them how it feels to be loved and appreciated, to show them the right way to love. I want to be the dad they can come to when they need advice, the dad they come to when they need help, the dad they can be vulnerable with. I know parenting is no easy task, but I want my kids to know that I will never leave them or give up on them, and I will be there for them to count on no matter what. I don't care how much you claim to be a real man, if you can't be there for your children, you have some work to do on yourself.

I want to show my kids what a healthy relationship looks like. I want them to experience being raised in a dual-parent, stable household - not a bunch of moving around. I want to get a nice house to raise them in. I want to be the cool dad my kids don't mind bringing around their friends, the dad they are actually excited to brag about to their friends. I want to show support in whatever they do, no matter what they choose to do. If they want to play sports, then we will figure out how to make them the best athletes. If they want to act, then we will get them in acting classes and plays. I'll encourage them to be great and reassure them they can do whatever they want in life. I want to guide them down a path for success. I don't want to force my kids into doing what *I* want them to do either. I feel like that can turn into resentment as they get older. So, helping guide them into trying different things to see what they love will be critical.

I don't want to shelter my kids from the real world, I think it's important to find a healthy balance of keeping kids clear of danger and negativity, but also let them witness the problems this world has going on, so they can make informed decisions, and know how to deal with issues of the world as they get older. You hear stories of kids that are over-protected, and they act out as they get older, because they feel so out of touch with reality. They end up rebelling, and experimenting with drugs and alcohol. Of course, there are certain things kids shouldn't witness, but nowadays, things are a lot different than when we were growing up. The things they show on TV, the music that is being played, social media, etc. - there isn't really much left for the imagination anymore. I think the most important thing is letting kids know what a healthy relationship looks like and understanding the difference between real life and what is on television and the radio. I know everything isn't as perfect as the movies, but you can make a kid's childhood as amazing as possible if you put the work in. You can keep them safe from toxic situations.

As a kid, I definitely had my fair share of things I shouldn't have witnessed or would rather not have gone through, both from my mom and dad. The physical abuse my mother dealt with, seeing her in and out of some pretty toxic relationships. We moved around a lot. I remember moving to Mississippi for a few months to live with a guy she was dating. He was abusive and started to put his hands on my mom, so one day while he was away, we packed up all of our stuff and drove back to Minnesota. We stayed at my aunt's house in the suburbs for a while before moving back in the city, just for her to meet a new guy and move us again. This time we moved to Florida with him to live on the beach. Just when we were getting settled in, he up and left us. We ended up staying in a shelter for a bit until my aunt sent us some money to catch a Greyhound bus back to Minnesota. So, we stayed with my aunt in the suburbs again for a bit, before moving back to the city so I could finish high school. My mother did an amazing job of raising me on her own. I wouldn't be the man I am today without her. She showed me what it is to be a loving God-fearing, and forgiving person. She taught me my work ethic. I think all the moving around that we did helped to make my decision to move to LA easier because I wasn't afraid of change. She just had a poor judgment of men in her life and it came from the brokenness that stuck with her from childhood.

I saw a good amount of things with my dad I definitely shouldn't have seen as well. I don't think he realized I knew what was going on. He may have thought I was too young or naïve, but I knew for sure. I saw drugs being used, drugs being sold, and prostitutes. I just never wanted to say anything because I knew my mom wouldn't let me be around him anymore if she knew. It wasn't all the time that I saw these things happen, just every once in a while. No excuse, but I just loved my father and wanted to be with him as much as possible, so I just brushed it off. My father wasn't intentionally trying to put me in bad situations or hurt me, he was just following a broken pattern that he came from. Both of my parents later apologized for the things I had to witness. My father used to tell me he was sorry all the time until the day he passed, I think my mother apologized to me yesterday about the things I had to see. They were forgiven a long time ago, and I always remind her that. I understand the lifestyles they came from, I understood they were never taught what was right. They were trying to figure it out the best they could. Experiencing both the good and the bad helped mold me to know exactly how I will raise my future kids.

Do you think it's healthy to keep your kids sheltered from life's problems? Why?

_____

_____

_____

_____

What excited you about being a parent? What fears do you have of being a parent?

_____

_____

_____

_____

What are some things you wish you had not experienced as a child that you want to make sure your kids don't experience?

_____

_____

_____

_____

CHAPTER NINE

GET HELP

GET HELP

Knowing what I know now, I think a lot more people in the world need to seek help through therapy, counseling, spiritual guidance, mentorship, even self-help books. Seeking at least one can make a lifetime of differences. I never realized that I had so many feelings bottled up that I needed to set free. My pride and immature thoughts convinced me otherwise. I believed that I had it all together, that my problems weren't that bad, and that talking to someone really wouldn't help me in any way. I don't think I knew anyone around me that has really took the initiative to get proper help either. My mother would always tell me she felt it would be best for me to see a therapist and talk about my childhood, but I thought I was fine. It wasn't until I hit rock bottom in my relationship that I realized I was far from fine. I had been crying out for help, and didn't even realize it. Now it makes sense, it doesn't matter how small an issue may seem, if left untreated, it can grow into something that can leave irreparable damage. A lot of adult's tendencies and issues stem from childhood problems that have been left untouched. It's ironic how it takes someone that doesn't even know us from Adam to put our life into perfect perspective. For me, I also needed to talk to a life coach that has been through similar experiences as myself in relationships, and has succeeding in life making the right choices. I needed to talk to a man that has learned how to be faithful and help other men understand what it takes. I needed someone to take a look at my career and give me some extra insight on how to take things up a notch. Everyone needs help in some way, shape, or form. No one is perfect, no one has life figured out. As you reach new levels in life, there are new things you must learn in order to grow even more, before you can be the teacher, you must be the student.

The first help I got was spiritual guidance. I went to my pastor, Pastor Touré for his advice on what he did to become whole, to overcome temptation, and to shift his entire life to walk for the Lord. The first thing I wanted to do before anything, was give my life to God. I had been feeling a sense of an inner battle for quite some time, and the final cheating situation was the breakthrough that my spirit had my crying out for. God was speaking to me about many aspects of my life - my strength against temptation, my confidence, my faith, some unhealthy habits that were holding me back from receiving my full blessings, such as drinking and watching pornography. I wasn't able to give my woman my all in our relationship because I was all over the place.

I knew that before I did anything else, I needed to center myself in God. My pastor let me know about the lifestyle he was living and choices he was making before he gave his life to the Lord. He talked to me about his infidelity, and how he got to a point in his life where he was sick and begging the Lord to heal him. He knew he had a calling on his life, and he knew breaking his control of temptation was the first step to align himself with God. He told me how he broke the news to his boys about the changes he was making in his life. He let them know that he wasn't going to keep doing the same things he did in the past. He had to separate himself from certain situations that could hinder his growth in any way. He gave me tips on how to heal spiritually through my break-up as well. He shared with me different books to read, including the bible and some good scriptures for healing, and encouraged daily prayer. I know not everyone believes in the same God - if any God at all, but there is a God. The proof is undeniable. We are not just put here on earth for no reason. We have all been put here to live out a purpose. The first step to bettering yourself and your life is getting on a spiritual frequency and understand how to tap into that purpose. Get as close to God as possible. In the Bible, Colossians 3:10 states, "And have put on the new self, which is being renewed in knowledge after the image of its creator," meaning renew yourself and live through the knowledge of God our creator. You may think you have it all figured out - I know I did, but if you are living with one foot in trying to see what you can get away with, it will only go so far. Everything in the dark eventually comes to the light. The ways of the flesh eventually creep up on us one way or another. For men, a lot of times it's temptation. Then, it's our anger, our pride, or ego. The best choice I made to put an end to all of these things is submit to my God.

The next step I took to get help was reach out to a psychiatrist. I needed some professional advice on relationships. I needed to understand why so many men are the way we are, why so many of us do the dumb things we do, and why did I let myself get to this point. I also knew I had a lot of pain from my childhood that I had bottled up inside. I had been avoiding talking to anyone about it, but I hit the end of the road, I needed to talk to someone and figure out what I was doing wrong, if it was deeper than just the excuse of me being a man. I needed to vent to someone and talk about all the things that I had been carrying with me all these years. I needed to talk to someone that wouldn't judge me, someone that wouldn't tell me what I wanted to hear just to make me feel good. Someone that would give me their honest opinion. Someone who deals with people in similar situations on a daily basis. I felt it was necessary for my growth, and I was right. She helped me put so many things into perspective. I was able to get a better understanding for my actions based off my subconscious, not even realizing what it was I was doing. I learned how my childhood was affecting me in my adulthood. She taught me ways to reprogram my thoughts and my actions. How to assess situations in my life from a deeper outlook. I learned to really take in every moment and think about why I approach it the way I do. If I'm looking at a female in a sexual way, I really stop and ask myself, *"What is it about this girl that is drawing me in? What is it that is attracting me to her or making me think sexually of her? What would happen if I were to sleep with her? What would I gain? What would my actions be afterward?"*

She taught me to think about the bigger picture in every situation before making a decision. It seemed so obvious, like how could I not have been thinking like this before?

The relief you gain from talking about your feelings is unreal. It's like a huge weight being lifted off of your shoulders. When someone else lays your life experiences and mishaps out for you, the picture seems so clear. Why had I been avoiding this for so long? I highly encourage every man to talk to a professional at some point, even if it's just one time. The stigma of being a man alone can carry so much stress. Having to be strong, hold in your emotions, having to fit in, having to prove yourself to other men, your sexuality...the list goes on. Talking about these things with someone that you know will not judge you can save you a lifetime of issues. It can also speed up the process of your growth and healing.

The third professional I connected with was my life coach, Tony Gaskins. I talked to him briefly early in my relationship when I got caught cheating the first time, but lost touch pretty quickly, and thought I was good on my own. This time around, I knew I needed to learn as much from Tony as possible. I knew that I needed to understand his transformation to fully help form my own transformation. At first, I was nervous to reach out to him again because I felt ashamed for messing up another time when he was trying to help guide me down the right path the first time, however I knew I needed to set my pride aside and fully connect now. I knew he would play a major role in my growth and new beginning. I was also losing my mind missing Liane so bad, and I needed his advice on how to handle myself. I planned on spending my entire life with her, and now she wanted nothing to do with me. I was blowing her phone up, showing up to the house unannounced, and begging for her to give me another chance. I was acting a damn fool. I honestly made it worse for myself. Forcing a situation only pushes someone further away from you. Tony helped me understand this better. He told me how he lost his girl when he wasn't living right, and he had to let her go and focus on bettering himself and getting himself whole. He let me know that I needed to just worry about myself right now and focus on healing myself, reprogram my mind, and realize that it is time to MAN UP. He ended up reconnecting with his girl a year later. They ended up getting married and they are still married until this day – they have been married thirteen years, to be exact.

Besides being a loving, faithful husband and father, he is super successful and understands how to maximize your potential in life to the fullest. Before my separation, I had already been feeling stuck in my career - the breakup only added to it. I needed someone to whip me into shape and rejuvenate my thinking process, I didn't want to make any more excuses for where my life was. He gave me so many tools for growth I am forever indebted to him. Anyone going through any stagnant feelings in life, any struggles in your relationship and/or career, I highly suggest seeking out a life coach. It will be one of the best decisions you can make.

I wish I had made these decisions to get help sooner, but I accept the timing in which it happened. I needed to go thru everything in my life the way I did before I got to this point. I had to see certain things and experience certain things in order to be able to put myself in other people's shoes, so I can help them grow. I know there is no excuse for bad behaviors, you just have to be ready and willing to get help and change. I want to encourage you, don't wait until it hits rock bottom to figure it out. Rather it's cheating, abuse, addiction, laziness, or low self-esteem. Whatever demon you may be dealing with, talk to someone, get proper guidance, hold yourself accountable to be the best version of yourself. Live for you and God only. It will be the best choice you have ever made. You will see everything else in your life fall into place the way it is supposed to.

Have you received help from a professional before? If so, what did you gain from it?

_____

_____

_____

_____

Do you believe the saying, "Once a cheater, always a cheater?" Or, can people change their ways? Explain.

_____

_____

_____

_____

_____

What do you feel your next step should be towards reaching your full potential?

_____

_____

_____

_____

CHAPTER TEN

YOU ARE THE MASTER OF YOUR OWN LIFE

YOU ARE THE MASTER OF YOUR OWN LIFE

I wanted to add in this chapter about changing your paradigm and manifesting because it has gotten me to every phase of my adult life, both good and bad. I have recently started to dig deeper into understanding the Law of Attraction, as well as all the other laws of the Universe. I used the Law of Attraction to get to where I wanted in my career without even realizing it. My burning desire for success and my career forced me to lay out a game plan to get it and not stop until I reached it. I always believed that I can be whatever I want in life, as long as I put the work in to get it and never give up. So, when I decided I would move to LA to become a famous entertainer, I already believed that's what I will eventually be. I am a poster child for the saying, "A dollar and a dream." I moved to LA with no money or car, only a dream and a burning desire to get it. It took me seven years before I got my big break in Hollywood, and once it hit, my career took off like a rocket. I was attracting things to me without even realizing it. But, the problem is not all things I was attracting were positive. I didn't understand a thing about how the Law really worked. I didn't understand the paradigm shift of the subconscious mind that must take place.

After my break-up I went on a search for help to make a full spiritual and mental transformation, and one of the best things happened to me. God put everything into place for me as far as who I needed to connect with, and what resources I needed to gain the necessary knowledge. I had to stay with my mom after moving out of the place me and Liane shared, because I had nowhere else to go. Luckily, I moved her to LA a couple years ago, and got her a nice home with extra space for me. I was down and out every single day, sick to death from the break-up, and one morning my mom was scrolling through YouTube, looking at positive affirmation videos and came across a Bob Proctor video. Bob was teaching on the Law of Attraction and shifting your paradigm. After watching this video, we watched a couple more hours of videos. I was shook, the light bulb came on in my head, and I understood everything so clearly. Not just about my life, but why so many people's lives are the way they are as well. As much as I attracted success to my life, I also attracted failures to my life. No matter how hard I wanted to be faithful in my relationships, I couldn't because I was worrying about not being a good boyfriend. My whole life, all I knew was men cheating, so it was ingrained in my subconscious. With so many things based off sex in the world, my mind was constantly consumed with thoughts about other women. Pornography, half naked-women all over social media, strip clubs, and music videos - mine included. Other rapper's music talking about having all type of girls, side chicks…the list goes on. I was subconsciously attracting my destiny to mess up. In my career, when things started going great, I would worry about my work slowing down, I would worry about going broke, I would worry about getting booked for certain gigs. There would be times where I would doubt my talents and my future. I wasn't fully aware of the power of manifestation. I was battling myself without even knowing it.

I ordered Bob Proctors book, 'We Were Born Rich,' along with Napoleon Hill's book, 'Think and Grow Rich,' and after reading these two books it put everything in perfect perspective. If you only read two books in your life, please read at least one of these books. Both of them are must-haves for understanding how to use the Law of Attraction in all aspects of your life.

We become what we think about most. It's so simple but it's true. If you take a look at some of the most successful people in the world, you will realize that the majority of them started with nothing. All they had was a burning desire to become rich and successful. They wouldn't let anyone tell them differently, they kept that image in their mind and then they figured out what they needed to do in order to make it a reality. As much as you can speak success and good fortune into your life, you can also speak poverty and misfortune. In the Bible, Proverbs 18:21 says, "Death and Life are in the power of the tongue; and they that love it shall eat the fruit of it." This means that whatever you think about and speak most, you will bring into your life. Have you ever noticed how many musicians have died at an early age who spoke about their deaths in a song at some point? It's trippy, but it's real. You must be very careful with the thoughts you allow to come into your head and the words you allow to come out of your mouth. The outcome of your life will begin with you shifting your paradigm.

Paradigm shift meaning: A fundamental change in approach or underlying assumptions.

We must make it a point to reprogram our subconscious mind to attract everything we want.

Look at the results in your life, and it will tell you what you think about most. Most people are consumed by worry, doubt, thoughts of lack, sickness, and debt. So many negatives. The thing about the Law of Attraction is even if you are always saying, "I don't want to be broke", or "I don't want to lose my job", or "I don't have enough money", or "I don't want to be a cheater", or "I don't want to be in an unhealthy relationship" - the Universe doesn't know the difference. It picks it up as what you want, that is the energy you put out, so it continues to feed it. You have to speak abundance into your life. You have to learn to speak as though you already have everything you want and need. Speak things into existence. I know it is hard to believe or understand, but if you take a second and think about it, it will make perfect sense.

We were put here to live in the image of God, to love and create. Have you ever noticed when things are going good in your life, things just keep getting better? When you are consumed in love, it seems like nothing in the world can stop you? Unless you start to worry that it might end, then you attract that end to you. Or, if you wake up on the wrong side of the bed, and don't fully recover from it, the day just keeps getting worse. We attract it all to us. Trust me, I know it's hard to manage every thought we have, but a great trick that is easy to learn is to work on having good feelings as much as possible. Write down things you are grateful for. Imagine yourself having everything you ever dreamed of and how you will feel having it. Think about living in abundance with zero lack. Close your eyes and picture yourself being the person you always imagined and how you would feel. If you want to manifest money into your life, write down an exact amount of money you wish to have. Create a burning desire to get that amount of money. The universe will start to put things in place for you to reach that goal. You may get an idea of a lifetime that pops into your head, or a crazy opportunity from a friend, or bump into someone on the street in the same field of work you are trying to get into. You will never know how it will come about, but it will come once you fully believe it and set your intentions on having it. If you really want to tap into manifesting, I highly suggest you watch 'The Secret' on Netflix.

Here's a true story for you: A friend of mine started the year off with a couple thousand dollars in the bank. He watched 'The Secret' at the beginning of the year, and decided he wanted to make a million dollars by the end of the year. He watched the secret every day for that entire year and shifted his mindset to abundance. Guess what? Financial opportunities came to him all year, left and right. He ended the year with over a million dollars in his bank. That's just one of many stories. All of the mentors in my life that changed their paradigm and decided to speak faithfulness, Love, and abundance into their life are all living amazing successful lives. They are in beautiful loving marriages and reaping God's blessings ten-fold. Since I have submitted to God, and walking in my purpose, speaking light into my life, the blessings have been off the charts. The beautiful thing about abundance is that it's unlimited. You can manifest the love of your life to you, the career of your dreams, the amount of money you want, and the person you want to become.

Follow these three steps to manifest whatever you want: 1.) Ask 2.) Believe 3.)Receive. First you have to Ask the universe for what you want. You must be specific with what you want. The more detailed the image you paint in your head of what you want, the easier it will be to attain it. Second, once you have asked for what you want you must Believe that it is already yours. Have faith that you will have it soon. Believe you deserve it and believe it is coming your way. This is a hard one because you must use your imagination to the fullest. The more you practice this, the easier it will get. The final step is to Receive it, feel the feelings of you already having it, imagine your feelings in the moment receiving it. Think about how amazing you will feel. Feel happy now, feel the joy now, feel the gratitude now, let your imagination run wild. You must let your positive energy overflow into the Universe. A good habit to help accelerate your manifestation is to meditate first thing in the morning for 5-10 minutes, and then again at night. During your meditation, focus on clearing everything out of your mind other than the things you want to receive. Focus on how you will feel having it. Picture yourself in that new car, or new home, or holding a stack of cash, or being with the love of your life. Focus on the feelings of happiness this brings you. Once you start to really live these three steps, you will start to see an amazing shift in your life. You will be addicted to only allowing positive thoughts to flow, protecting your energy from negative people. Keep working on blocking out as much negativity as possible. Manifest the life of your dreams. You are the master of your own life.

Write five things you want to manifest beginning with, I am happy and grateful now that…

For example, "I am happy and grateful now that I made $100,000 this year."

_____

_____

_____

_____

_____

_____

_____

Write down the exact amount of money you want to make this year and date it. Then write three things you can do to immediately get started on reaching that goal.

_____

_____

_____

_____

_____

Write down five things you are grateful for in your life. Look back at these five things every day and repeat them to yourself.

_____

_____

_____

_____

_____

_____

_____

_____

CHAPTER ELEVEN

THE SPOTLIGHT IS BRIGHT

THE SPOTLIGHT IS BRIGHT

Success in the wrong hands can be a dangerous thing. Fame along with success in the wrong hands can be even more dangerous. We see it all the time, the amount of celebrities that reach a certain status of fame and lose their minds. They fall victim to drug abuse, alcohol abuse, sexual scandals, and even suicide. Fame or no fame, any type of notoriety can leave you susceptible to a world of trouble if you are not cautious. The fame can get to your head so easily, you can become cocky, arrogant, and self-centered. Every temptation you can imagine is amplified. Imagine being able to do whatever you want and get whatever you want. The possibilities are endless. When you are famous, you get everything for free, literally everything. From clothes, shoes, jewelry, food, liquor, cars, you can get into any night club anywhere in the world, free flights, hotels, I mean the list goes on. You have people doing whatever you tell them to do just to be around you. Women dying to get a picture with you. For a lot of men, the biggest sell is the amounts of women throwing themselves at you. This type of attention and praise can become an addiction if you are not in the right mental state.

Here's the thing, a lot of people in the world have low self-confidence, issues with feeling accepted, and the need to feel acknowledged. A lot of people are lacking self-love and acceptance. Believe it or not, there are a lot of men that have low self-esteem and feed off of the praise of other men, or the superiority feeling they get from hooking up with new women. Most of the time, as men, we don't even realize we are doing it. We find ourselves doing things out of our usual nature to impress other people. Most of the time, for famous people or people with some type of notoriety it's drinking, doing drugs, or behaving a certain way with women. The crazy part is a lot of the people we are so eager to impress could really care less about you. This sometimes only adds to the problem because once you realize it, it leads to trust issues, and you feel like no one really cares about you as a person, but only your name and status. It can lead to trying even harder to impress people or be well-liked. It's unfortunate, but there are so many celebrities or people of notoriety that were chasing fame only to be able to patch up these insecurities, to finally be accepted and loved. Those people usually end up worse off after reaching it.

When I moved to Hollywood from Minnesota in 2006 to get into the entertainment industry, I had a burning desire to succeed. There was also a part of me that wanted to become a famous actor to make my father happy. His lifelong dream was to be an actor, and since he never saw it through, I wanted to carry that legacy on for him. I never had any issues in the women department, so for me, that part of fame wasn't a selling point; however, it definitely made it sound sweeter at the time. From experiencing living in Hollywood, women definitely became a bigger reason for getting fame.

I was living with four of my buddies in a one-bedroom apartment in Inglewood, California. We were all aspiring actors and rappers with our sights set for the spotlight. We were all barely twenty-one, living in LA, away from our families back home. We didn't have real jobs. We made our own schedule and did what we had to do to make money to pay our bills. We got paid to be background actors in movies and TV shows. Most of the time, we were all booked together on the same gigs. Most of the gigs, we had more down time than actually work, so all we would be doing is goofing off and trying to pick up girls that were working with us. Aside from acting, all of us did music. We had a rap group consisting the four of us called *Forward Movement*. If you want to get a vision of what we had going on, feel free to look us up on YouTube. Please don't judge me. We would print out copies of our mixtapes and we would sell them for $10 each everywhere - from the sets we worked on, to Santa Monica beach, to Target parking lots. These would pay our bills and we would also be able to meet new girls at the same time. We would set up performances at small sports bars all around the city to try to build our name and make a little bit of money on the side. To be honest, I don't remember there ever being more than ten or twenty people at any of the shows, so we weren't making much money or fans in the process. These were major ego-killers for all four of us constantly. Between being denied roles we were all auditioning for on a daily basis, being background actors sitting in the shadows of working actors, and our music not growing like we wanted it to, we gained a sense of hunger for some kind of love and acceptance.

All four of us were single and in party mode, but we didn't have much money at all. So, when we would try to get into the nightclubs, we would get denied at the door, and couldn't afford to pay the cover to get in. We would see all the famous athletes and rappers walking right in with groups of women, and man - that was a major ding to our egos! We watched them walk in with ease, as we sat outside on the ropes. We wanted that kind of love and acceptance. We thought the only way to go about getting it immediately was to fake it 'til we make it. We finally got into one of the main clubs and we got connected with a promoter that was one of the biggest in the scene. Now mind you, we were all attractive and we knew how to dress, so we looked like we could have had money or been somewhat successful. So, we lied to this promoter and told him we were newly signed artists on Lil Wayne's record label 'Young Money.' This got us in the door with him, and we were in the clubs on a consistent basis, living this new fake life to be accepted. Trying to uphold this image we had painted in our head that we thought would make us cool enough to fit in and stay in. Don't get me wrong - at the moment we were living our best life. We had no worries in the world, you couldn't tell us nothing - drinking every night, parties and after-parties until six in the morning, and attractive women everywhere. Thank God I didn't do drugs, but I saw so many celebrities doing them, it blew my mind. The promoter was bringing us girls left and right telling them we were signed to Lil Wayne's label, so now we were lying to these girls to get them to like us as well.

We carried this lie on for quite some time before eventually telling our promoter buddy that we got dropped from the label, and asked if we could start promoting with him. During the time of club promoting, I met so many celebrities and its crazy how lost so many are. They didn't care about finding love because they can't trust anyone, and they think everyone is after their money. They have girls begging for a night with them, so they are sleeping around town. I worked a few nights a week and I would always see the same celebs out every night getting drunk, picking up new girls and leaving. To us, this was normal - it was the lifestyle we were living, but amplified. I see why they call Hollywood the Devil's playground. You get sucked into temptation so easily. Everything is all about pleasure of the flesh. The thing about the Devil is, he feeds off of your weaknesses. If you are getting notoriety and fame, and you are weak in temptation, he's going to latch on and feed into it. If you have a hard time saying no, you will keep finding yourself in situations that are hard for you to turn down. You find yourself spending more money to keep up with other celebs. Spending money to impress people. Buying bottles in the club, buying expensive jewelry, and designer clothes. Eating out every night at extravagant restaurants, the list can go on for days.

Once I came off of filming America's Next Top Model, and found myself with this new-found fame, I started to experience everything on an even higher level. The attention I was getting from women, new friendships I was making with celebs, the money I was starting to make, and new spending habits were all new to me. I was becoming consumed in the praise I was getting from everyone, I never had large amounts of money before, so I was spending like crazy, I was drinking every night. A lot of nights, I drank to the point of blacking out. I always had my foot halfway in with my faith in God, so if I started going too far down the wrong path, the spirit would speak to me. There would literally be times where me and my boys would be out partying all night, drinking, hooking up with girls, and get up and go to church the next morning like nothing happened. It's crazy looking back at it - how lost I was at times, how caught up in the life I would find myself. But, I got to see why so many people with fame and success lose it all so easily. Not everyone can control themselves and pull themselves out of this lifestyle. A lot of people don't see anything wrong in living this life. Or, they think there is no hope to change the way of living.

If you are not grounded in God, it is so easy for you to slip into the negative dynamics of Hollywood. Don't get me wrong, I am beyond blessed to be living out my dreams. To be a working Model, Actor, Musician, and there are a ton of other amazing things about the industry. It is a huge accomplishment to have made success out of my journey. I don't want to scare you away from success or reaching whatever dream you are chasing. I just want to warn you about the negative lifestyle that can suck you in real easy, if you are not aware. If you are not in the right place with God. If you do not love yourself and are not whole. Whatever way of life you are moving in now, the fame and notoriety will only amplify it. If you are living a blessed, prosperous, life things will usually tend to get better. If you are making a ton of sinful choices, chances are the Devil will present you with even more opportunities.

I know many entertainers that stay away from the negative side of things. Some who know how to balance their lives without getting pulled down to sin. Some who are married and faithful and have no urge to give into any of the temptation in Hollywood, who have learned how to do their work, build their platform and stay away from trouble. If you are seeking fame or any position of notoriety, I highly suggest you sit down and be real with yourself. Decide what it is you are *really* looking for in life. What are you looking to gain from it? Is it money? Power? Respect? Attention? Whatever your goal is, make sure you are working on your armor, so you are ready to stand strong when the tests come. No matter what goal you are chasing, trust and believe the tests will come. Be confident in who you already are as a person. Be grounded in your faith. Don't let the status go to your head, and don't feel the need to do anything to impress people or to advance in your career. Seek to impress God only. Focus on how you will use your status to better your life, not set yourself back. It's fun to go out with friends every now and again, but don't let yourself slip into an unhealthy pattern of chasing temptations. And trust me, there is no easier way of falling victim to it than when you have some type of major status. The spotlight is bright, you can let it shine through you or burn you out. The choice is yours.

Why do you think people let fame and success go to their head?

_____

_____

_____

_____

What can you do to remain humble once you reach a high level of success?

_____

_____

_____

Write down 5 good traits about yourself that your peers admire about you.

_____

_____

_____

_____

CHAPTER 12

YOUR BOYS CAN WAIT

YOUR BOYS CAN WAIT

Oftentimes, our friends are our biggest influences in our life, both good and bad. We look to them for advice, for approval, and for acceptance. We expect our friends to ride for us no matter what, and vice versa. As guys, we never want to let our boys down, we don't want to let them see us vulnerable, we always want to seem like we are strong and in control. We feel like we have to be a certain way, or do certain things for them to accept us. It's a pack, no one wants to be the first to stray away from the pack. Our boys come first no matter what. BROs over...well, you how the saying goes. As we get older, we realize that's not it at all, or maybe not even as we get older, but as we *mature*, we understand that's just being BOYS and not MEN. Once you become a MAN, you realize you can't do the same things you did when you were younger. No more running the streets all hours of the night, chasing girls, sleeping around, and Lord knows what else. You grow up, you find a woman to start a family with, and she becomes priority - your family becomes priority. In the Bible, Proverbs 18:22 says, "He who finds a wife finds a good thing, and obtains favor from the Lord." Commitment is a key factor in becoming a man, and it usually starts with your relationship. Once you can commit in a relationship you commit in all other areas of your life. You ever notice how a majority of the most successful men in the world have a wife by their side? Your boys are no longer just friends, your friendships become a brotherhood, your boys become your brothers, and they become the ones that won't judge you for any decisions you make in life, only support you and have your back no matter what.

The problem is not all BOYS turn into MEN. Some boys want to stay boys for a lifetime, never grow up, never face true responsibilities in life, and never commit to anything. Rather it involves being caught up in fleshly pleasures, being complacent, or scared of change. Some men just don't want to let go of their "freedom," they want to be able to come and go as they please, they think that is the real meaning of being a man. This could be a result of not knowing any better, or it could be the absent relationship of their father, or some other childhood issues. Whatever it stems from, I know one thing for sure, - that's the easy path. It's easy to stay single your entire life, it's easy to stay out late drinking all night. It's easy to browse through dating apps and hook up with new girls all the time, with no strings attached. It's easy to sleep in Sunday mornings, skip church, wake up and watch some football. It's easy to carry unhealthy old habits into new situations. Anything that is unhealthy for us usually comes easy. Commitment to anything in life is work, turning your dreams into reality is work, lasting relationships require work, changing old patterns that weren't good for us is work. But, the beautiful thing is the payoff for anything that is hard work is beyond rewarding – it is life changing.

I've lived my entire life chasing fleshly pleasures. That was all I knew. That was what I thought life was about. That's not it at all. Chase the approval of God, and by doing so, abundance will come. Your true passions will transpire, and you will find a burning desire to pursue your true happiness. I am on a new journey in life, and I encourage you to join me. I encourage you to take a look at your life, look at the way you are living, and the way you have been living. What is it you are chasing in life? Is it the approval of people, or is it the approval of God? For the longest, I was searching the approval of people, but today I am proud to say the only approval I seek is that of God. My Boys are my brothers, and we support each other through everything with no judgement. We ride or die for each other, but on this path to Manhood and being a man of God, they can wait. Your boys can wait. They will have to respect that you can't do some of things you once did, you are not that person anymore. They may not understand it right away, or believe the change, but as time goes on and they see how serious you are, they will learn to accept it. As you all grow as Men, God-willing, they will follow suit in finding their full purpose and potential. We are brothers, we must lift each other up together.

LETTER TO MY BOYS

My boys, we had some good times in life, didn't we? I could write an entire book on the stories we've had alone. Maybe I will one of these days. Now I know most of us didn't have the father figures we needed in our lives, or guidance we probably should've had. We had to figure it out as we went throughout our journey of life. I think we all turned out pretty good, given the circumstances. If I had to change anything in my life, I wouldn't, I take the good with the bad and the bad with the good. To some of the fights and fall-outs some of us have had over the years. To the road trips, cross-country drives from Minnesota to California. The last minute, late-night drives from LA to Las Vegas with $20 in our pockets just to chase some girls. To our one-bedroom apartment in Inglewood full of air mattresses and futons. Waking up to forty-ounce beers and oatmeal cream pies for breakfast. What about the highlight of our week doing background work on music video sets to make $150 and meet some new girls? So many parties, too many parties. The performances and club hosting's all over the world. The list goes on and on. So many life experiences and I wouldn't have asked for a better group of guys to go through it with. So many lessons I've learned over the years and I'm thankful for every last one. All of you have supported me and had my back through every phase of my life, so I know as I take on this new path, it won't be any different. I've lived a certain way for so long, I feel it is now time for me to change courses. Stop chasing things that are going to keep me from being whole and focus on what God truly has for me. I am looking forward to new experiences and the blessings that life has to offer all of us from here on out. I pray I am able to not only help my brothers in my inner circle in every way possible, but also help my brothers in the entire world. So, here's to new beginnings and new memories. May this next chapter of our lives be the best chapter.

Write a letter to your friends.

_____

_____

_____

_____

_____

_____

_____

_____

_____

_____

_____

_____

_____

_____

MY TRUTH

CHAPTER 13

LETTER TO GOD

LETTER TO GOD

Dear Lord,

Thank you for all of the blessings in my life. Thank you for good health, for my family, my friends, thank you Lord for my mother. Thank you for my career, the ability to do what I love on a daily basis and reach millions of people. Lord, continue to let your light shine through me as my life on this Earth continues, let my voice be an echo of yours, let my presence be a shadow of ours. Thank you for never abandoning me, no matter the situations. Thank you for the lessons that I have learned throughout my entire life. Forgive me for my sins, forgive me for the choices I have made that I am not proud of. Thank you, Lord for waking me up today, for waking me up and changing my outlook on life, for accepting me to walk in your name. I know the challenges we face oftentimes seem so drastic and unbearable, but I understand that in order to give our all to you, we must be depleted with nothing left in ourselves to rely on. I ask you Lord to keep my father's spirit by your side and watching over me and my mother, let him be my guardian angel the remainder of my time on this Earth. Lord, I know that my battles are still just beginning, and I have so many more tests to face, but I ask you to give me the knowledge and strength to get through it all. I know as long as I'm with you, nothing can defeat me. Lord, I come to you and ask you to make me one of your soldiers on this Earth, let me spread your name and the abundance that comes with it. Give me the strength to help as many people as possible, rather it be financially, emotionally, or spiritually. Let me continue to be a great leader and continue to lead by example. I know that we don't have to be a certain way to be accepted by anyone, as long as we are accepted by you, that's all that matters. We can stand strong in the face of temptation and come out with a win. Lord, please put forgiveness in the hearts of any women I have hurt in my past. I was broken and you know I did not mean it intentionally. I pray you keep them safe from harm and bring them the love they truly deserve. I pray you put forgiveness in the hearts of anyone else I may have hurt in my life. I can honestly come to you today saying I love myself and I forgive myself. Lord, I ask you to continue to put the right people in my life that will continue to help my career prosper, help my relationships prosper, help my every day well-being prosper. I understand that we were put here to live in the image of You as kings, to have whatever our hearts desire in accordance to Your name. I ask you to continue to bless me abundantly and continue to let me be a blessing to others. Watch over my friends, whatever they are dealing with in life, I know you will speak to them and show them the right way to get through it. I ask you to watch over my family, keep them healthy and in good spirits. Watch over my mother, keep her healthy and well and allow her to live a long, fulfilling life alongside me. I ask you to watch over Liane and her family. Put love and forgiveness in her heart. Keep them filled with abundance and good health. I know we don't understand the way you force us to learn lessons here on Earth sometimes, but I accept them all. I know that things must happen the way they do because it is how you already had everything designed. I ask you Lord, to put your blessings on this book and let it spread across the world to touch as many people as you see fit. Let it change the hearts and minds of many men and give women an insight that they can use in life as well. Thank you, lord for loving me unconditionally, I will continue to maneuver in Love unconditionally as well. In your name we pray, Amen.

Made in the USA
Las Vegas, NV
12 May 2022

48811956R00059